Field Guide to the
NORTH AMERICAN
JACKALOPE

by Andy Robbins

ISBN: 987-1-59152-303-1

Published by Caput Mortuum Books, Ranchester, Wyoming

Cover illustration: American Jackalope (front), Western Jackalope (back).

You may order extra copies of this book by calling Farcountry Press toll free at (800) 821-3874.

Produced by Sweetgrass Books
PO Box 5630, Helena, MT 59604; (800) 821-3874
www.sweetgrassbooks.com

Produced and printed in the United States of America.

Elusive. Otherworldly. Beautiful.

These words—and *many* more—can be used to describe one of North America's most enigmatic creatures: the jackalope. The purpose of this field guide is to provide the reader with a scientifically accurate description of the jackalope, its habits and habitats, as well as the history of the species and its North American subspecies. Popular jackalope myths will also be examined to gain further understanding of jackalope behavior. We hope you find this guide an indispensable introduction to the fascinating world of the jackalope!

What is a Jackalope?

A jackalope refers to both males and females of a distinctive species of hare, a mammal that looks like an oversized rabbit. Jackalope males grow antlers from the frontal bone of the skull that resemble miniature versions of those more commonly found on deer. Both male and female jackalopes have oversized ears that provide excellent hearing as well as elongated rear feet that allow for superior speed and traction on the ground. Jackalopes are typically larger and more powerfully built than their more common rabbit or hare counterparts. Opportunistic omnivores, they can be found in pairs or free-ranging groups throughout North America.

All jackalopes are wild, yet wise. Mysterious, yet knowable. Magical, yet *real.*

Are you ready to meet the jackalope?

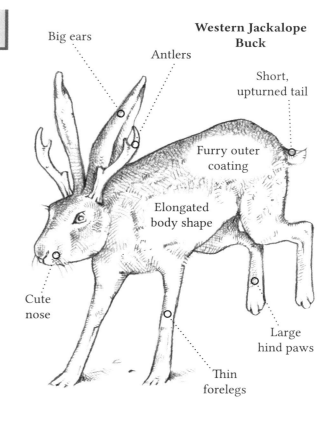

Western Jackalope Buck

Big ears

Antlers

Short, upturned tail

Furry outer coating

Elongated body shape

Cute nose

Large hind paws

Thin forelegs

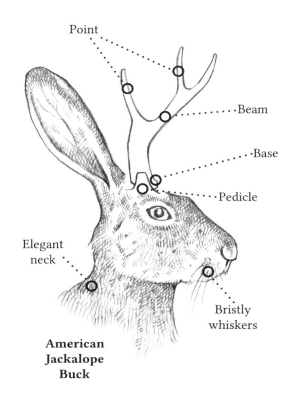

Point

Beam

Base

Pedicle

Elegant neck

Bristly whiskers

American Jackalope Buck

Jackalopes can run so fast that all you'll see is a puff of dust on the horizon.

Jackalopes have been clocked at speeds in excess of 55 mph and can cover as much as 25 feet in a single leap. Though the list of animals that eat hare includes coyotes, foxes, and eagles, the jackalope rarely falls prey to these predators since its speediness makes it extremely difficult to catch. Stories of jackalope quickness may be exaggerated, but there's a good deal of truth to them.

A jackalope at full speed.

FACT

5

Artist's rendition of a proto-jackalope.

Origin of the Jackalope

The term "jackalope" is a misnomer. In appearance, the antlers of a male jackalope bear no resemblance to the horns of the antelope (a colloquial term referring to the pronghorn), and instead look like those found adorning animals of the deer family. But to call the jackalope a "jackadeer" would be equally inaccurate. Genetically, the jackalope is not related to either of these two mammals; instead, it is classified among the lagomorphs with hares, rabbits, and pikas.

Jackalopes are grouped in the same zoologic family (Leporidae) and genus (*Lepus*) as other hares, but are a separate species (*cornutus*, meaning "horned"). Fossil records from Asia during the early Eocene Epoch reveal that during this period the lagomorphs broke away from rodents to become the rabbits, hares, and jackalopes found on Earth today. While the jackalope remained true to its hare roots for a time, a freak genetic mutation occurred roughly 30 million years ago, endowing the jackalope with its characteristic antlers. Though odd-looking, these additions proved advantageous in contests of physical strength and so . . . they stuck. Not long after their antlers appeared, jackalopes spread across the globe, their various subspecies eventually separated by continental drift.

So, where did the first true jackalope live? The short answer is that we don't know for sure, but evidence points toward Asia—India specifically—as the origin of the species. Fossil records do exist for the jackalope in North America, with specimens dating back as far as the Middle Miocene, or 14 million years ago. In Europe, the history of the jackalope is less clear, though illustrations of the creature appear frequently in medieval manuscripts. Hares with antlers are also mentioned in folklore from Africa, Asia, and Central America.

Wherever it originated, the jackalope's impressive antlers, lightning-fast feet, and flexible diet helped it find a foothold in the North American ecosystem where it has coexisted peacefully, more or less, with jackrabbits and other lagomorphs for millennia. Though genetically similar save for the recessive trait that causes antler growth, jackalope subspecies do not interbreed with their more common relatives, possibly due to divergent mating practices.

A jackalope fossil, Converse County, Wyoming.

A Gallery of Jackalopes Throughout History

"Lepus Cornutus," Antonio Tempesta, 1600.

"Al-Miraj and Dragon," Turkish.
Walters Manuscript, 13th Century.

Animalia Quadrupedia et Reptilia (Terra),
Joris Hoefnagel, 1580.

Porte-feuille instructif et amusant pour la jeunesse,
Jacob Xaver Schmuzer, 1805.

Animalium Quadrupedum Vivae Icones,
Adriaen Collaert, 1612.

Animaux Du Monde Réel,
Pierre Joseph Fausse, 1842.

*Angenehmer und Nuetzlicher Zeitvertreib mit
Betrachtung Curioser*, Johann Daniel Meyer, 1750.

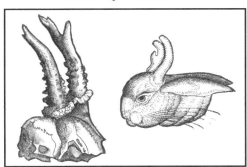

Historia Animalium Quadrupedum,
Conrad Gesner, 1602.

The jackalope was born when a herd of deer and several jackrabbits were forced to live in a cave together during a particularly harsh winter.

This tall tale attempts to explain how the jackalope got its deer antlers and, while more titillating to imagine than the slow plod of evolution, isn't possible. These two mammals are too far apart genetically to produce offspring.

Jackalopes are the result of an outlandish lab experiment.

In a story originating at Texas A&M University, a group of entrepreneurial scientists attempted to create a hybrid animal suitable for both hunting and eating. They finally succeeded by crossing a white-tailed deer with a jackrabbit. The result was set free (or escaped) onto the plains, where it quickly multiplied. While it may look like jackalopes were created in a lab, they are instead the product of time and genetic mutation.

FICTION

North American Jackalopes of Antiquity

While the focus of this field guide is the living jackalopes of North America, a look back in time can be enlightening. Prehistoric jackalopes were numerous and varied. Some contributed attributes still found in jackalopes today: the extra incisors of the Sabertooth Jackalope or the insulated undercoat of the Woolly Jackalope, for example. Certainly none of today's jackalopes would be as successful or good-looking without the perseverance of their forerunners, a small sampling of which is presented here!

Bearded Timber King *(cornutus silvarex)*

The massive antlers of this jackalope might appear too heavy to tote, but they were hollow and lightweight. It's believed the Timber King knocked its antlers against trees to create catchy beats for other jackalopes to enjoy. A once-plentiful creature of the primeval forest, evidence suggests the Timber King may have been revered as a god by Paleo people. Depicted in cave doodles as a supernatural beast, early humans created fertility fetishes from Timber King antlers.

11

Sabertooth Jackalope (*cornutus draconius*)

The Sabertooth Jackalope's teeth weren't much different than the incisors found in modern jackalopes; they just grew super fast. Chewing was required to keep these "fangs" in check, so the Sabertooth Jackalope gnawed on the bark of trees in beaver-like bursts. This jackalope was the first to possess peg teeth, likely as back-up biters in case of breakage. Sabertooth fossils are often found in Southern Californian tar pits, indicating this jackalope may not have been very bright or might have just had a thing for tar.

Woolly Jackalope (*cornutus cardiganius*)

Like the mammoths that once trundled across Ice Age steppes, this jackalope grew a thick coat to help it survive fluctuating temperatures. Chemical analysis from Woolly Jackalope carcasses frozen in permafrost indicates that their hair would have made excellent sweaters. Though the modern Northern Jackalope bears some similarities to the Woolly Jackalope, they are only distantly related in a very hard to explain genealogical way.

Trivial Deermunk
(*cornutus parvadiabolii*)

Though fossil evidence is scarce, experts speculate that the Trivial Deermunk may have been an amniote—an animal that lays eggs instead of giving live birth—making it a rarity among mammals. Small, bucktoothed, and fluffy, this early jackalope wasn't as wimpy as it appeared. He used his sharp antlers to poke the toes of anything that came too close.

Great Plains Megalope (*cornutus megamaximus*)

A giant among its kin, mobs of this massive jackalope thunder-thighed across central North America's tall-grass prairies 10,000 years ago. Equal in size to many primitive predators, its rake-like antlers allowed it to fend off attacks with ease. The Megalope's size may have spelled its doom, however. It reproduced in great numbers and overgrazed the plains, resulting in mass extinction.

Jackalope Evolutionary Tree

Kingdom: Animalia

Phylum: Chordata   Family: Leporidae
Class: Mammalia   Genus: *Lepus*
Order: Lagomorpha   Species: *cornutus*

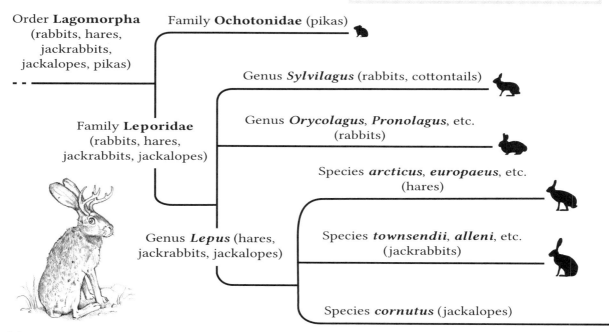

Order **Lagomorpha**
(rabbits, hares,
jackrabbits,
jackalopes, pikas)

Family **Ochotonidae** (pikas)

Genus *Sylvilagus* (rabbits, cottontails)

Family **Leporidae**
(rabbits, hares,
jackrabbits, jackalopes)

Genus *Orycolagus*, *Pronolagus*, etc.
(rabbits)

Species *arcticus*, *europaeus*, etc.
(hares)

Genus *Lepus* (hares,
jackrabbits, jackalopes)

Species *townsendii*, *alleni*, etc.
(jackrabbits)

Species *cornutus* (jackalopes)

14

North American Jackalope Subspecies

Lepus cornutus americanum

Lepus cornutus occidentis

Lepus cornutus anglicus

Lepus cornutus aquabestia

Lepus cornutus murahkanis

Lepus cornutus canadensis

Lepus cornutus minima

Contemporary Jackalopes

The following pages of this guide contain detailed descriptions of the seven known living subspecies of the North American Jackalope. Though some are currently endangered, all can still be viewed in their native environments by the persistent observer. To minimize identification frustration, familiarize yourself with these breeds before heading into the field!

Note: Numerous exotic jackalope subspecies are present throughout the world and can be found on every continent with the exception of Antarctica. Please refer to *Jackalopes of the World* by Andy Robbins for further information on lagomorphs beyond the scope of this guide.

American Jackalope
(*Lepus cornutus americanum*)

American
Jackalope Buck

The most well-known of the jackalope subspecies, the American Jackalope is found from the forests of Saskatchewan to the central grasslands of the United States, as far east as Illinois and as far west as California. This subspecies measures 22-26 inches in length, and has a white tail several inches long. Color varies from dark brown to greyish-brown with a pale grey underside. Weight varies depending on latitude, from 5 to 10 pounds, and up to 15 pounds during record wild berry seasons. Males annually grow a pair of branched antlers, beginning in spring and lasting until midwinter, when they are shed.

Size Comparison

Geographical Distribution

Picture perfect pose: If you see a jackalope featured on a postcard, it's likely an American Jackalope, the unofficial mascot of the species.

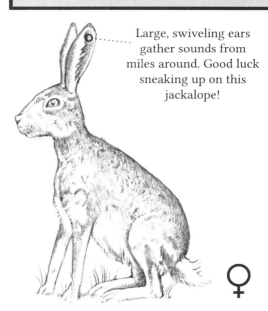

Large, swiveling ears gather sounds from miles around. Good luck sneaking up on this jackalope!

♂

♀

17

Western Jackalope
(*Lepus cornutus occidentis*)

Western
Jackalope Buck

The Western Jackalope lives in an area that encompasses the southwestern United States and portions of Mexico, including the Baja peninsula. Weighs between 5 to 8 pounds and measures over 2 feet in length. Its coat is a dark brownish-yellow with a grey or white underbelly and a black-topped tail. The antlers of this jackalope are smaller than those of its northern counterparts, though bucks are known to be aggressive, perhaps to compensate for the size difference. The Western Jackalope lives in sagebrush-dotted grassland and amidst desert scrub where it eats nearly everything save for rocks and sand.

Size Comparison

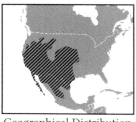

Geographical Distribution

Frontiersmen used Western Jackalope antlers for eating implements when forks weren't available!

♂

Population: 3000+
Status: Vulnerable
Lifespan: 8-15 years
Length: 18-24 inches

Full of blood vessels, the Western Jackalope's ears help regulate body temperature.

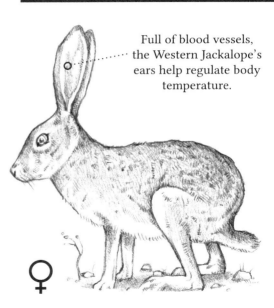

♀

Lesser Eastern Jackalope
(Lepus cornutus anglicus)

Lesser Eastern
Jackalope Buck

Once common throughout the Eastern United States and around the Gulf of Mexico, the Lesser Eastern Jackalope saw dramatic population declines during the 20th century due to over-trapping for pet markets. It is now considered endangered. Weighing 1 to 3 pounds, this jackalope is greyish-brown with a white underside. Antlers of the male Lesser Eastern Jackalope tend to be of the spike variety. Despite an ear-piercing cry when threatened, this jackalope is known to be easily domesticated once in captivity. Feeds primarily on grass. The Appalachian Jackalope is a slightly larger, more disagreeable variant.

Size Comparison

Geographical Distribution

These horns don't look like much, but be careful: bucks often hone them to fearsome points on trees!

Population: Less than 1000
Status: Endangered
Lifespan: 5-8 years
Length: 13-15 inches

The Lesser Eastern Jackalope's scream is said to sound like a cross between an eagle cry and a cat yowl.

♂

♀

21

Coastal Lowland Jackalope
(Lepus cornutus aquabestia)

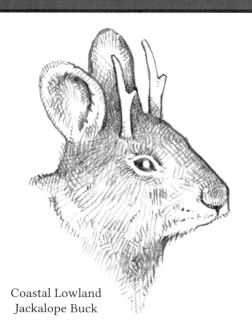

Coastal Lowland
Jackalope Buck

The Coastal Lowland Jackalope lives in the cypress swamps and cattail marshes of the southern United States from Virginia to Alabama. Though this jackalope is an Olympic-caliber swimmer in the water, its short legs aren't as quick on land; instead of hopping, it walks, a trait unique among jackalopes. Prefers ocean view properties but is content as long as there's water nearby and aquatic roots to eat. Once established, the Coastal Lowland Jackalope builds permanent, hair-lined cottages from grass and leaves. You'll need sharp eyes to spot this jackalope: it often hides in the water with only its nose, ears, and tiny antlers breaking the surface!

Size Comparison

Geographical Distribution

Population: 500
Status: Endangered
Lifespan: 5-10 years
Length: 14-18 inches

♂

The oily outer layer of this jackalope's coat wicks away moisture to help her stay dry and comfortable. Slick!

The Coastal Lowland Jackalope has been known to swim across miles of open water to eat a single, ripe blackberry!

♀

23

Russet-necked Jackalope
(*Lepus cornutus murahkanis*)

Russet-Necked
Jackalope Buck

An increasingly rare species, the Russet-Necked Jackalope has been hunted nearly to extinction across much of its initial range in the south-central United States where it is coveted as a stew ingredient. The male's distinctive antlers branch only at a considerable length; females sometimes have small, pointy antlers. Considered a pest in many localities due to its tendency to help itself to unattended crops, gardens, and fried foods. It is also known for its particularly shrill call, irritating even to other jackalopes. Wily and irascible, the Russet-Necked Jackalope is as wild as they come!

Size Comparison

Geographical Distribution

Population: Less than 250
Status: Critically Endangered
Lifespan: Unknown
Size: 13-18 inches length

Both males and females have a distinctive red band of fur around their necks that give the subspecies its name.

Russet-necked does may also have horns. Look out now!

Northern Jackalope
(*Lepus cornutus canadensis*)

Northern
Jackalope Buck

The Northern Jackalope (also known as the Jack Pine Jackalope) makes its home in the boreal forests of North America, from Newfoundland to Alaska with satellite colonies in the Sierra Nevadas and the Rocky Mountains. Weighs 3-6 pounds and measures 15-22 inches in length. The Northern Jackalope grows white fur in the winter to camouflage itself. Both male and female Northern Jackalopes grow short, flattened antlers that are not shed until spring. These stylish antlers are also practical: the Northern Jackalope uses them to clear the extensive network of trails it maintains in winter and to push aside snow while foraging for plant material.

Size Comparison

Geographical Distribution

Dressing down: A lightweight, brown coat provides camoflauge during summer months.

FAST FACTS

Population: 5000+
Status: Least Concern
Lifespan: 10-12 years
Length: 15-22 inches

Thick, white winter fur helps the Northern Jackalope survive temperatures as low as -40°F!

♂

♀

Pygmy Jackalope
(*Lepus cornutus minima*)

Pygmy
Jackalope Buck

The smallest of the jackalopes, the Pygmy Jackalope weighs a mere pound and measures 9 to 12 inches in length. Found in sagebrush environments in an area that includes parts of Montana, Utah, Idaho, Oregon, and central California. Ears and hind legs are noticeably shorter than those of other jackalopes. It is the only member of the species that digs burrows for living quarters. Its spartan diet is believed to consist almost exclusively of flower blossoms and juvenile crickets. A rare creature of which little else is known.

Size Comparison

Geographical Distribution

The ultimate homebodies, these jackalopes often stick to a territory of less than 1000 square feet.

FAST FACTS

Population: Unknown
Status: Vulnerable
Lifespan: Unknown
Length: 9-12 inches

Pygmy Jackalopes are always found (when they're found at all) in pairs. 2 cute!

Antlers

All male jackalopes—and in a few cases, female jackalopes—grow an annual set of antlers. Velvet-covered antler growth begins in early spring and continues through late summer, at which time the velvet (a soft skin layer that facilitates antler development) falls away to reveal a pair of bony antlers. Antlers are shed after rutting season, usually in December or January. Young male jackalopes may grow buttons (small ossified knobs) instead of antlers during their first year. Size of antlers depends on many factors including age, nutrition, and genetics, and may appear as spikes (single, pointed growths) or branched, multi-pointed racks, dependent on subspecies.

The antlers of a jackalope buck are used for sparring with other breeding males to establish a dominance hierarchy. These matches are often fierce, with the sounds of battle echoing through the sagebrush as two jackalopes lock together in fearsome combat. Rarely is blood drawn, but so great is the strength of a jackalope buck that serious injury or death can result from such dueling. So, too, has the jackalope buck been known to use its antlers to bruise the skin—and ego—of a human who gets too close for comfort.

Two bucks clash with antlers.

Branched
antlers

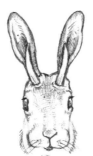

Spike
antlers

Button
antlers

Non-typical
antlers

Jackalope Antler Variations

Antlers in
velvet

Recently shed
antlers

Shope Papilloma Virus (SPV)

SPV, also known as cottontail rabbit papilloma virus, affects rabbits and hares in North America. The virus causes keratinous carcinomas (horny growths) around the face and head which can become large enough to prevent the host from eating. Hares infected with SPV have been cited as a possible source for the jackalope "myth," but the difference between an animal infected with SPV and a healthy jackalope buck will be obvious to an observer in the field. SPV creates abnormal, grotesque growths, while typical jackalope antlers are symmetrical, well-formed, and situated in pairs just below the animal's ears. Jackalopes, it should be noted, appear to be immune to SPV.

Hare infected with SPV

Jackalope with normal antler growth

Original illustrations by Ernest Thompson Seton documenting SPV in rabbits, 1916.

Commonly found on rabbits, hares, and jackalopes, the rabbit tick contributes to the spread of skinborne viruses like SPV as it moves from animal to animal.

32

One should wear protection when looking for jackalopes.

Jackalopes are territorial and will protect their mates and young. Males are known to charge with their antlers when threatened. The best solution, it's been said, is to outfit one's legs with lengths of stove pipe. While this method might be effective against jackalope assaults, it is too cumbersome to be practical. In reality, quick reflexes and a pair of thick pants should be adequate against all but the most persistent attack.

PARTIAL FACT

Note: If antlers are not present, a jackalope can be positively identified by *very carefully* checking inside its mouth. While many lagomorphs have a set of peg teeth (short, stumpy incisors located behind the first incisors) jackalopes have a sharp, fully-formed second set of incisors behind the first, much like those of a shark.

Jackalope

Hare

33

The Jackalope Diet

Jackalopes are generalized foragers. Since their habitats range from mixed grass prairies to alpine meadows to desert shrublands, their diet is necessarily varied. Grasses, flowering plants, buds, twigs, and cacti are all fair game, as are cultivated crops such as alfalfa, corn, and barley. Jackalopes have been observed feeding on small game such as frogs, snakes, mice, and even unwary rabbits when particularly ravenous. Jackalopes can forgo water for entire seasons, with some desert subspecies observed to drink only rarely over the course of several years. Even with respect to moisture gleaned from plants, this trait is highly unusual and as yet not fully explained by science.

FACT OR FICTION?

Jackalopes love whiskey.

Lore holds that jackalopes are attracted to whiskey. So much so, in fact, it's said the liquor can be used as bait to capture the animals. Field tests have shown that such claims are valid. When offered whiskey, jackalopes showed a keen interest, often travelling for miles to investigate. Drinking the liquor was another story, however; jackalopes appeared attracted to the smell, but stopped short of imbibing, sensing perhaps that the grain content of the drink wasn't worth the inconvenience of the alcohol.

FACT

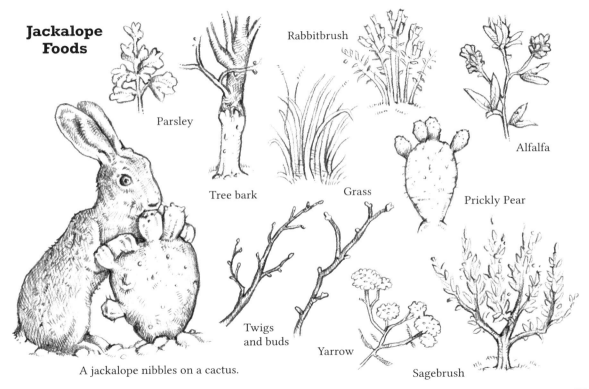

Jackalope Foods

Parsley

Tree bark

Rabbitbrush

Grass

Alfalfa

Prickly Pear

Twigs and buds

Yarrow

Sagebrush

A jackalope nibbles on a cactus.

35

Family Life

Jackalopes mate for life, though how they select their partners remains largely a mystery. Jackalope mating rituals may include elaborate, choreographed dances or other courtship activities, but with the exception of sparring, no such behaviors have been observed in the wild. Jackalope couples do stay together for the majority of their lives, however, sharing a living space, foraging territory, and even parenting responsibilities (though some jackalope bucks are more attentive than others).

Jackalope homes are simple affairs. Like other hares, the jackalope makes use of a form (a slight depression beneath the sheltering branches of a bush or tree) as an all-purpose shelter and nursery. Here, jackalope leverets (babies) are born with their eyes open and are capable of immediate and rapid flight. Despite this precocial cunning, most leverets look to their parents for guidance and protection for

A doe in a form.

a year or more. Jackalopes live solitary lives after leaving their mother's care until reuniting with other jackalopes during the annual rut to spar or take a permanent mate.

Unlike their lagomorph relatives, who are prolific reproducers, jackalopes tend to have small litters of only 1 to 3 leverets with litters further limited to one per year. In an environment shared by jackrabbits and jackalopes, this discrepancy makes it apparent why the former is the more plentiful of the two.

Jackalope milk has medicinal properties.

It has been said that consuming jackalope milk cures many illnesses and may even been an aphrodisiac. Unfortunately, due to the difficulty in obtaining jackalope milk samples, this claim has been impossible to verify.

UNKNOWN

A pair of jackalope leverets.

Jackalopes only mate during lightning storms.

Legends say that jackalopes conceive solely during storms with significant atmospheric electricity. While apocryphal, such accounts do contain a grain of truth. Jackalopes have shown a preference for evenings of heavy cloud cover or turbulent weather in which to conceal their mating rituals. Conversely, extreme temperatures, particularly heat, will delay the jackalope rut. Recent data even suggests that lunar cycles may play an active role in jackalope reproduction.

PARTIAL FACT

A jackalope warning cry.

Communication

Jackalopes use an assortment of sounds to frighten predators, send warnings to other jackalopes, and broadcast challenges or mating interest. The jackalope alert system is so effective that it makes ambushing a jackalope extremely difficult if another is nearby. Often mistaken for a human scream, the terrifying shriek of a frightened or injured jackalope can be heard for several miles. More pleasant vocalizations appear to indicate romantic interest; observers of these furtive noises claim they resemble singing. In other instances, jackalopes will imitate the sounds of different animals. Coyote howls and dog barks are common jackalope mimicries; both are intended to mock or confuse predators. Meadowlark birdsong and owl hoots are favorites used to soothe young. More bizarrely, jackalopes have been known to repeatedly imitate cellphone ringtones in order to frustrate hunters.

A jackalope calls to a prospective mate.

FACT **OR** FICTION?

Jackalopes understand human speech, repeat phrases, and can even sing songs.

One of the most enduring jackalope stories centers around jackalopes listening to a song being sung around a campfire and then eerily joining in from the shadows. Cowboys swear they've heard voices in the darkness harmonizing to their favorite tunes—in tenor voices, no less. Witnesses even claim that the jackalope's song can calm an entire herd of cattle. These tales may have some basis in fact. Jackalopes are adept mimics, and some of their vocalizations have been described as pleasing to the ear, while others, like the crying of a human baby, seem intended to deceive. Whether jackalopes understand human speech is another question altogether.

PARTIAL FACT

A jackalope joins two cowboys in song.

Lifespan

Under optimum conditions, jackalopes can live for unusually long periods of time. While a typical jackrabbit might expect to live up to 5 years in the wild, a jackalope can survive for twice that long, or even longer, depending on subspecies. The age of some trophy American Jackalope bucks has been estimated at more than 20 years.

39

Locating a Jackalope

There is no foolproof way to find a jackalope. Jackalopes are crepuscular (active at twilight) and nocturnal, though they can occasionally be found during daylight hours if the conditions are acceptable. A quiet, sunset walk through an undeveloped area where other lagomorphs are known to live is a great way to determine if jackalopes also inhabit the region. Once on the ground, there are a few signs you can look for to locate a jackalope.

All jackalopes have furry feet that lack pads so they don't always leave discernable tracks. Snow cover can provide better opportunities for tracking. In larger subspecies, hind feet leave tracks 5 inches or more in length, while front feet are less than half the size. Jackalopes have several distinct gaits, including a hop, a distance-devouring gallop, and the rarely-seen swagger.

Male jackalopes will occasionally create scrape marks in the dirt or grass. These markings range from simple lines to curiously complex patterns and may be produced to mark territory or simply as joyful artistic expression. Boisterous jackalope bucks may also scratch or scar trees with their antlers.

Hop

Gallop

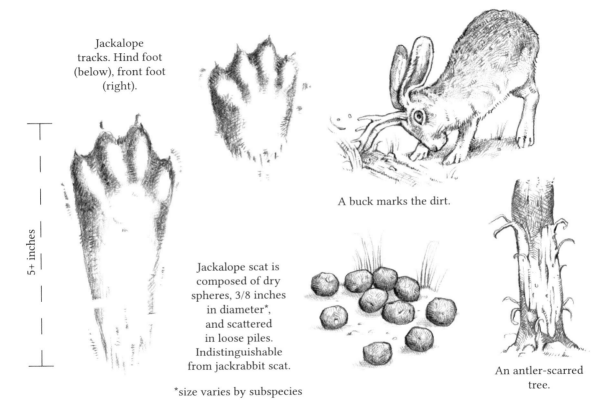

Jackalope tracks. Hind foot (below), front foot (right).

5+ inches

A buck marks the dirt.

Jackalope scat is composed of dry spheres, 3/8 inches in diameter*, and scattered in loose piles. Indistinguishable from jackrabbit scat.

*size varies by subspecies

An antler-scarred tree.

Helpful Hunting Hints

The chase is on!

Bring a Dog: A human may pass within inches of a jackalope and never see it. Bringing a dog improves the chances of flushing jackalopes from hiding spots. Don't worry about your dog catching and harming a jackalope. The odds of this happening are zero—dogs just aren't fast enough!

Take a Drive: One great way to look for jackalopes is to take a moonlight drive. Jackalopes often gather on road surfaces, and it's easy for beginning observers to spot them on pavement. Choose a promising area and start cruising. But not too fast! You don't want to hit any jackalopes! A friend can shine a flashlight from the passenger seat, but local law enforcement may notice. Be prepared with a story about a missing pet or grandparent.

Have a Seat: A tried and true method for patient jackalope hunters. This approach is deceptively simple. Find a spot at dusk, sit down, and wait. It might be awhile. Spotting a jackalope in this way is often a life-changing and spiritual experience.

Note: This is not a trick to play on friends, but a valid research technique.

Rookie Mistake: Don't Fall Asleep!

Jackalope merchandise

In Popular Culture

Antelabbit. Rasselbock. Warrior Rabbit. Stag Bunny. *Jackalope.*

For over a century, the jackalope has captured the imagination of cowboys, biologists, tourists, and hunters. The jackalope embodies, in its own freakish way, the mystery and ruggedness of the American West. Adopted by many states and municipalities as a quirky symbol, this curious creature has generated revenue through postcards, stuffed animals, and the preserved pelt of the animal itself.

Though townships from Montana to Texas claim the jackalope, no place factors so prominently in jackalope history as does Wyoming. Reports dating from the early 19th century document the jackalope befuddling the state's first trappers and cowboys. As settlers arrived, large groups of jackalopes (known as mobs) could be seen stampeding across the plains. The first known specimen of a jackalope wasn't made public until 1932, however, when a fine buck was taken by Douglas Herrick of Douglas, Wyoming and put on display in in a local hotel. This jackalope caused

Shoulder mount buck

so much excitement that it wasn't long before hunters hoping to score a jackalope were scouring the wilderness with a passion that persists to this day.

Likewise, the jackalope is still a point of civic pride in several places, most notably Douglas, Wyoming, which is known as Jackalope City and the "birthplace" of the jackalope, and in South Dakota, a state with strong ties to the jackalope and a large producer of commercial jackalope taxidermy.

Jackalope statues at Wall Drug, South Dakota (left) and Douglas, Wyoming (right).

Fakes and Forgeries

A prize as majestic as the jackalope is bound to command a premium price. To fill this lucrative market, entrepreneurs create many skillful forgeries using assorted lagomorphs as bases. Harvesting a jackalope for oneself remains the best way to acquire an authentic specimen, but for many this isn't an option, making the secondary market the only alternative. Presented here is a sampling of common fake jackalopes to better inform the buyer.

Extreme trophy racks are suspect and may be appropriated white-tailed deer antlers or even plastic.

Jackalopes have antlers, not horns, so any outfitted with antelope horns are fabrications. No variation of this sort occurs in nature.

Sabertooth hares are believed extinct. All specimens of this sort should be met with skepticism.

Extra tall, curled, or spiral antlers may indicate an exotic breed or, more likely, a forgery.

Unilopes are fictional creatures. May be an animal affected with SPV (page 18).

Jackalopes with canine teeth are the work of creative taxidermists.

A Rogues' Gallery of Fake Jackalopes

Hunting and Conservation

Since the antlered hare's "discovery," the jackalope has become a grail for the big game hunter, and the thrill of successfully stalking one is said to surpass that of pursuing the most savage African beast. Until seeing one in the wild, many consider the jackalope nothing more than a comical cryptid (an animal not proven to exist). As such, successfully harvesting a jackalope represents the taming of the unknown, making it easy to see why this creature has had a target on its back since man entered the picture!

Jackalope populations have been managed unofficially in recent years to support the burgeoning jackalope taxidermy industry, with jackalope ranching operations finding modest success in Nebraska and eastern Washington. The jackalope, however, is as yet unrecognized by the United States Game and Fish Department. No hunting regulations for jackalopes exist beyond those outlined for jackrabbits, and, due to obvious similarities, the jackalope often falls prey to hunters unwilling or unable to differentiate between the jackalope and the more common rabbit and hare species. Further study is required to determine what regulations, if any, should be imposed so that future generations will be able to enjoy the jackalope.

The state of Wyoming attempted to regulate jackalope hunting by issuing a license for a single year in 1938. This license was the first and last of its type in the United States.

The Story of the Antlers: A Jackalope Folktale

Long ago, Warrior Hare lived in the sagebrush with his brother, Brother Hare. Like all hares back then, they both had fine sets of antlers. Warrior Hare was the strongest and fastest of all hares. He sparred against the other hares with his antlers, and his victories won him great honor.

Brother Hare, however, was lazy. He spent all day growing fat. He was envious of the admiration Warrior Hare received, but to Brother Hare it seemed like too much work.

Now Deer and Brother Hare spent a lot of time together, mostly eating.

Petroglyphs, Emery County, Utah

In these days, Deer had no antlers at all, and the more he looked at Brother Hare's antlers, the more he wanted antlers too. "He doesn't use his anyway," Deer thought to himself.

As Deer thought this, a sly smile crossed his lips. "Brother Hare," he said, "I know a way that you can make a reputation for yourself with only a minute's worth of work. We will race to the river. If you beat me, you can brag to the other hares and they will call you a great warrior. And if I win . . . you must give me your antlers."

This sounded good to Brother Hare—except for the last part. He loved his antlers. Still, winning a race against Deer would bring him much honor. "Deer eats even more than I

47

do," he thought, "so he *must* be slow." And so, Brother Hare agreed.

The two animals began their race. Brother Hare, who was out of shape, tried to keep up, but Deer easily reached the river first. And so, exhausted and feeling foolish, Brother Hare gave his antlers to Deer, who immediately placed them on top of his own head and bounded away into the brush, pleased with his craftiness.

When Warrior Hare returned home, he was taken aback. "Where are your antlers?" he gasped. Disgraced, Brother Hare told him that he had lost his antlers to Deer.

And this is why, to this day, some hares have antlers and some do not. And this is also the story of how Deer got antlers of his own.

—Author Unknown

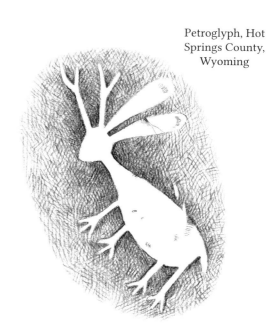

Petroglyph, Hot Springs County, Wyoming